my first book of
TELLING THE TIME

On the clock face the long hand points to the minutes, the short hand points to the hour. Sometimes on clocks and watches there is another hand which goes round the face very quickly, it is called the second hand.

There are 60 seconds in a minute.
A second is as quick as a wink.

There are 60 minutes in an hour.

There are two types of clock, one with a face and hands, and one that just has numbers called digits. Some digital clocks show 12 hour others show the full 24 hours in a day.

This is 2 o'clock in the afternoon on a 12 hour clock.

This is the same time on a 24 hour clock.

These clocks show all 24 hours in a day.
The time from 12 midnight to 12 noon is called
'A.M.'. From noon to midnight is called 'P.M.'.

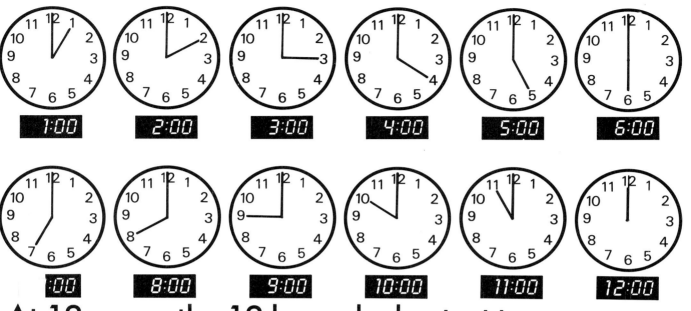

At 12 noon, the 12 hour clocks start to go
round again. The 24 hour clocks just go on
adding up to 24.

At 12 midnight a new day begins, and all the
clocks start again.

Here is a story about an exciting day out.
Learn about time from the little clocks
in each picture.

The twins are fast
asleep. It is 7 o'clock.

Here comes the milkman. It is 7.15, a quarter past seven.

7:15

Here comes the postman with the letters and a parcel. It is 7.30, half past seven.

7:30

Mother calls: "Get up, it's late, it is 8 o'clock. We are going out today."

The twins jump out of bed and run to the bathroom to get washed.

Hurry up twins, get dressed straight away. Pull on your socks, put on your shoes, it is 8.15, a quarter past eight.

Breakfast is on the table ready to eat. It is 8.30, half past eight.

"Grab your coats, I will lock the door. The bus will be here at 9 o'clock," says mother.

They get to the bus stop out of breath. Here comes the bus, right on time.

"Where are we going?" ask the twins. Mother says: "Wait and see." The bus stops at the railway station at 9.15, a quarter past nine.

The train arrives at 9.30, half past nine by the station clock. Climb aboard, and off we go.

The train speeds on through the countryside, past woods and fields and over bridges. Half an hour goes by. It is now 10 o'clock.

At last the train stops at a little station and everyone gets off.

The ticket collector has a big watch that says 10.15, a quarter past ten.

The twins and their mother leave the station and start walking down the lane.

It was a lovely walk down the lanes, through a village, and past a church with a clock that said 10.45, a quarter to eleven.

"Here we are at last," says mother. It is a park with lots of animals. "We open at 11 o'clock," says the man at the gate, "you're just on time."

First they see a hippo.

Then a zebra with lots of stripes.

They make friends with a monkey...

...but not with the camel.

Then it was 11.45, a quarter to twelve. "Come on," says mother, "there's something I want you to see."

The keeper is feeding the sea lions at 12 o'clock.

12:00

At 12.30, half past twelve, he feeds the penguins with fish from a bucket, and the twins help him.

12:30

"Look! It's 1 o'clock," says mother. "It's our feeding time now. We will have a picnic at that table over there."

It is afternoon. The 24 hour clock now says 13.00, the thirteenth hour of the day.

Mother says: "It is 1.30, half past one. I will sit here and you can look around for an hour by yourselves."

First the twins go to see the parrots and the other lovely birds.

At 2 o'clock they go to Pets Corner to play with the baby animals.

2:00   14:00

When they get back to mother, she says: "You are just in time to see the dolphins at 2.30, half past two."

"Oh dear," say the twins, looking at their watches. "It is 3 o'clock and there is still so much to see."

`3:00` `15:00`

They see a big brown bear.

A tiger that growls at them.

And a lion that is fast asleep.

`3:45` `15:45`

They see a giraffe, as tall as a house…

…and a big bad tempered rhino.

4:30   16:30

"Have we time to see the snakes and the crocodiles?" ask the twins. "Yes," says mother. "If we are finished by 5 o'clock.

"You two must be hungry," says mother. "We have time for a quick snack before we leave for home."

When everyone has finished eating, the clock says 5.30, half past five.

"Now we must hurry to the gates," says mother. "The park closes at 6 o'clock."

"Goodbye," says the man at the gate. "I hope you have enjoyed your visit."

6:00   18:00

They get back to the
station at 6.45, a quarter
to seven. Mother says: "We
have to wait 15 minutes
for the 7 o'clock train."

`6:45`   `18:45`

Here it comes, right on time.

`7:00`   `19:00`

After their journey by train and bus
they arrive home at 8 o'clock just as
it is getting dark.

The twins go straight upstairs to get washed and ready for bed.

Mother brought them a hot drink. "You must be tired," she says. "It is 8.30, half past eight."

By 9 o'clock they are both fast asleep. It has been a long busy day!

The twins are asleep, but the clocks go on counting the time up to 12 o'clock midnight.

10:00 **22:00**   **11:00** **23:00**   **12:00** **24:00**

Can you fill in the missing times from these clocks?

7:30   **:**   **8:45**   **:**

10:00   **:**   **11:30**   **:**

12:15   **:**   **3:00**   **4:45**